Facts About the Siberian Husky

By Lisa Strattin

© 2019 Lisa Strattin

Facts for Kids Picture Books by Lisa Strattin

Little Blue Penguin, Vol 92

Chipmunk, Vol 5

Frilled Lizard, Vol 39

Blue and Gold Macaw, Vol 13

Poison Dart Frogs, Vol 50

Blue Tarantula, Vol 115

African Elephants, Vol 8

Amur Leopard, Vol 89

Sabre Tooth Tiger, Vol 167

Baboon, Vol 174

Sign Up for New Release Emails Here

http://LisaStrattin.com/subscribe-here

Monthly Surprise Box

http://KidCraftsByLisa.com

Contents

INTRODUCTION

The Siberian Husky is a medium-sized working dog breed. They originated in Northeast Asia where they have been bred for sled-pulling, guarding, and companionship.

CHARACTERISTICS

The Husky howls instead of barking. They are also known to be escape artists, which means they are capable of digging under, chewing through, or even jumping over pretty high fences.

They need the frequent companionship of people and other dogs, and their need to feel as part of a pack, as well as their hunting instinct, is very strong.

APPEARANCE

A Siberian Husky's coat is thicker than most other dog breeds. It has two layers: a dense undercoat and a longer topcoat of short, straight guard hairs. This protects the dogs against harsh Arctic winters, and also reflects heat in the summer. Their thick coats require regular brushing.

They come in a variety of colors and patterns, usually with white paws and legs, facial markings, and tail tip marking. Their eyes are an almond shape and can be brown, blue or black, and, in some dogs, two different colors.

These dogs will often curl up with their tails over their face and nose in order to provide additional warmth. This position is referred to as the "Siberian Swirl."

REPRODUCTION

Typically, females should not be bred until they are at least 2 years old, and should stop around 9 years old. She will have a litter of between 4 to 9 pups and will suckle them for about 6 weeks, then they are weaned and old enough to eat solid food.

LIFE SPAN

The average lifespan of the Siberian Husky is between 12 to 15 years.

SIZE

Males are usually between 20 and 24 inches tall at the withers and weigh between 35 and 65 pounds. Females are generally smaller, growing to between 19 to 23 inches tall at the withers and weighing between 30 to 60 pounds.

HABITAT

Their natural habitat is a cold, northern climate, but that doesn't mean they can't survive in warmer conditions. Quite the opposite in fact. Even though they have a thick double coat to help withstand harsh weather, they have now become a popular breed in virtually every corner of the globe. They do need some room to run and enjoy being outside. But they can live wherever you do!

DIET

There are many commercially prepared dog foods and treats that will be good for your Husky. You can make a choice at your local pet store or even at the nearest grocery.

TEMPERAMENT

Siberian Huskies are free-spirited and typically good-natured with people. They are athletic, playful, and light on their feet. They love being outdoors and require significant daily exercise, especially in cold weather.

SUITABILITY AS PETS

The Siberian Husky is a great pet. As with all dogs, some are more temperamental than others, so it is a good idea to watch how your pet acts around strangers and children so that you can let visitors know how best to interact with your Husky.

COLOR ME

COLOR ME

COLOR ME

COLOR ME

COLOR ME

COLOR ME

COLOR ME

Please leave me a review here:

http://lisastrattin.com/Review-Vol-261

For more Kindle Downloads Visit Lisa Strattin Author Page on Amazon Author Central

http://amazon.com/author/lisastrattin

To see upcoming titles, visit my website at LisaStrattin.com– all books available on kindle!

http://lisastrattin.com

PLUSH SIBERIAN HUSKY TOY

You can get one by copying and pasting this link into your browser:

http://lisastrattin.com/PlushHusky

MONTHLY SURPRISE BOX

Get yours by copying and pasting this link into your browser

http://KidCraftsByLisa.com

Made in the
USA
Middletown, DE